EASTERN EUROPEANS

Samovar
urn used in Eastern Europe,
especially Russia,
for boiling water for tea

IMMIGRATION AND THE AMERICAN WAY OF LIFE

Geologically speaking, the continent of North America is very old. The people who live here, by comparison, are new arrivals. Even the first settlers, the American Indians who came here from Asia about 35,000 years ago, are fairly new, not to speak of the first European settlers who came by ship or the refugees who flew in yesterday. Whenever they came, they were all immigrants. How all these immigrants live together today to form one society has been compared to the making of a mosaic. A mosaic is a picture formed from many different pieces. Thus, in America, many groups of people—from African Americans or Albanians to Tibetans or Welsh—live side by side. This human mosaic was put together by the immigrants themselves, with courage, hard work, and luck. Each group of immigrants has its own history and its own reasons for coming to America. Immigrants from different regions have their own way of creating communities for themselves and their children. In creating those communities, they not only keep elements of their own heritage alive, but also enrich further the fabric of American society. Each book in *Recent American Immigrants* will examine a part of this human mosaic up close. The books will look at some of the most recent arrivals to find out what they are like and how they fit into the whole mosaic.

Recent American Immigrants

EASTERN EUROPEANS

Jodine Mayberry

Consultant
Roger Daniels, Department of History
University of Cincinnati

Franklin Watts

New York • London • Toronto • Sydney

Developed by: **Ω Visual Education Corporation Princeton, NJ**

Maps: Patricia R. Isaacs/Parrot Graphics

Cover photograph: © Bob Daemmrich

Photo Credits: p. 3 (L) Cynthia Matthews/The Stock Market; p. 3 (M) John Eastcott; Yva Momatiuk/Woodfin Camp & Associates, Inc.; p. 3 (R) Jeff Greenberg; p. 8 The Bettmann Archive; p. 11 PhotoWorld/FPG; p. 13 (T) Topham/The Image Works; p. 13 (B) Topham/The Image Works; p. 15 UPI/Bettmann; p. 16 The Bettmann Archive; p. 18 Porterfield-Chickering/Photo Researchers, Inc.; p. 21 ARCHIV/Photo Researchers, Inc.; p. 25 Erwin Shuh/Gamma-Liaison; p. 28 The National Archives; p. 30 The National Archives; p. 33 Richard Younker; p. 34 Frank Keating/Photo Researchers, Inc.; p. 36 John Albok Collection of the American Hungarian Foundation; p. 37 The National Archives; p. 40 Derek Berwin/The Image Bank; p. 42 Jim Anderson/Black Star; p. 44 Dennis Brack/Black Star; p. 46 Jasmin/Gamma-Liaison; p. 47 Esaias Baitel/Gamma-Liaison; p. 49 Alon Reininger/Contact Stock; p. 50 John Chiasson/Gamma-Liaison; p. 53 Patrick Piel/Gamma-Liaison; p. 54 Camera Press/Globe Photos; p. 56 Ira Wyman/Sygma; p. 57 Brad Markel/Gamma-Liaison; p. 58 Novosti/Sovfoto; p. 59 Manuela Duppont/Gamma-Liaison; p. 61 Geoff Govf/The Image Bank.

Library of Congress Cataloging-in-Publication Data

Mayberry, Jodine.
Eastern Europeans / Jodine Mayberry.
p.   cm. — (Recent American immigrants)
Includes bibliographical references and index.
Summary: Recounts how Eastern European refugees and displaced persons—many of them Jews—arrived in America after World War II to begin new lives and contribute their skills and learning to their new homeland.
ISBN 0-531-11109-1
1. East European Americans—Juvenile literature.   2. Europe, Eastern—Emigration and immigration—Juvenile literature.   3. United States—Emigration and immigration—Juvenile literature.   [1. East European Americans.   2. United States—Emigration and immigration.]   I. Title.   II. Series.
E184.E17M39   1991
973'.04—dc20   90-12995 CIP AC

Contents

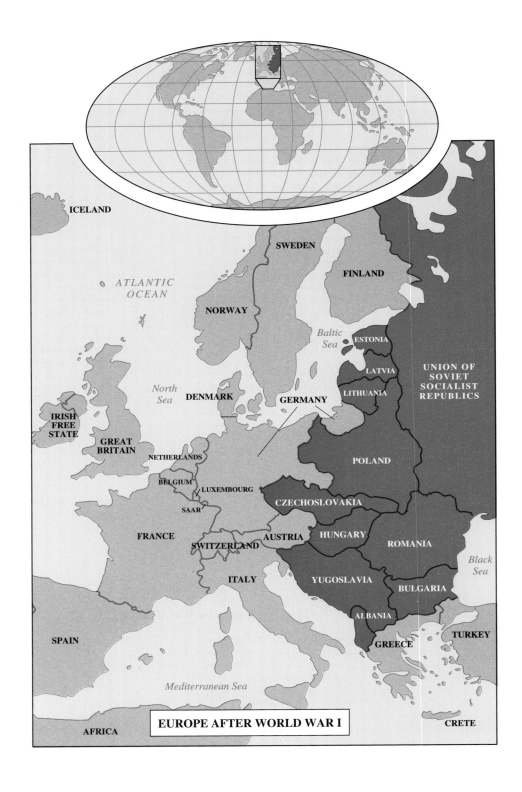

ICELAND

ATLANTIC
OCEAN

SWEDEN

NORWAY

FINLAND

Baltic
Sea

North
Sea

DENMARK

ESTONIA

LATVIA

LITHUANIA

UNION OF
SOVIET
SOCIALIST
REPUBLICS

IRISH
FREE
STATE

GREAT
BRITAIN

GERMANY

NETHERLANDS

BELGIUM

LUXEMBOURG

SAAR

POLAND

CZECHOSLOVAKIA

FRANCE

SWITZERLAND

AUSTRIA

HUNGARY

ITALY

YUGOSLAVIA

ROMANIA

Black
Sea

BULGARIA

ALBANIA

SPAIN

GREECE

TURKEY

Mediterranean Sea

EUROPE AFTER WORLD WAR I

CRETE

AFRICA

Between the Wars

The ancestors of millions of Americans came from Europe. The earliest colonists—after the American Indians—came from Spain, France, Holland, and the British Isles. This does not count the slaves from Africa, who were, after all, unwilling colonists. For more than two centuries, people from northern and western Europe—England, Scotland, Ireland, Germany, and the Scandinavian countries—immigrated in large numbers to America. They made English the national language and brought with them the seeds of American government, law, and culture.

Late in the nineteenth century, the pattern of European immigration began to change. Millions of people from southern and eastern Europe also started immigrating to America. These immigrants included Italians, Greeks, Poles, Russians, Hungarians, and eastern European Jews. This book examines three main ethnic groups from eastern Europe: Poles, Hungarians, and Soviet Jews. For the most part, the book focuses on immigrants from these groups who have come to America since World War II.

THE EARLIER IMMIGRANTS

Before World War I, millions of immigrants came to America from eastern Europe. Between 1870 and 1914, 2 million Poles and 485,000 Hungarians immigrated to the United States. During the same period, more than 2 million Jews arrived from eastern Europe, 90 percent of them from Russia.

These immigrants were poor, landless farmers and working-class people who were driven from their native lands by war, revolution, famine, and tyranny. They chose to come to America because it was the land of opportunity and freedom. It was a place where people could earn a good living and live without fear.

Most of these immigrants settled in America's northeastern and midwestern cities and went to work in factories and mines.

New York City's Lower East Side became a haven for immigrants from eastern Europe. Many set up shop on the street, as in this scene from 1910.

They contributed enormously to the growth of the United States as a major industrial nation.

EASTERN EUROPE AFTER WORLD WAR I

The nations of eastern Europe have a long history of turmoil. Some nations, such as Poland and the Baltic states of Estonia, Latvia, and Lithuania, were weaker than their neighbors. They were periodically invaded and annexed by stronger nations, usually Germany or Russia. National borders in eastern Europe have changed often in the last two centuries. People there identify themselves as belonging to ethnic groups mainly on the basis of their language or religion. A family of Hungarians may have grown up in a village that is now part of Poland, but they think of themselves as Hungarians because they speak Hungarian. Jews, however, may speak Polish or Russian, but most identify themselves primarily as Jews.

After World War I, the map of eastern Europe changed drastically. The war broke out in 1914, with Great Britain, France, Russia, and Italy—called the Allies—on one side. Germany, Austria-Hungary, and Turkey—called the Central Powers—were on the other side. The United States entered the war on the Allies' side in 1917. Germany was defeated in 1918. Revolutionaries overthrew the Russian czar in 1917 and established a socialist government. Then, in October of that year, early Communists, called "Bolsheviks," toppled the new government. In 1922, The Union of Soviet Socialist Republics was established.

After the war, the victorious Allies remade the map of Europe, creating new nations—Czechoslovakia, Yugoslavia, Estonia, Latvia, and Lithuania—and re-created an independent Poland. The independence of these nations would be short-lived, however. The Soviet Union made them satellites after World War II.

THE GOLDEN DOOR SLAMS SHUT

The poem on the Statue of Liberty reads, "I lift my lamp beside the golden door." The door had remained open for three centuries, but by 1920, most Americans were ready to slam it shut. Millions of immigrants had arrived. They came not only from Europe but also from China, Japan, and the Philippines. They performed the most dangerous and back-breaking jobs. In many ways—language, religion, customs, appearance—they were very different from other Americans. Many people believed that these new immigrants were taking jobs away from Americans. Others thought wrongly that the new immigrants were Communists or socialists out to over-throw the government. This prejudice against foreigners is called "nativism." Nativism is the attitude that America should be only for Americans.

THE IMMIGRATION ACT OF 1924

Many Americans pressured Congress to pass laws to keep out new immigrants. The Immigration Act of 1924 reduced the number of immigrants who could enter the United States each year to about 150,000. It also set quotas limiting the number of immigrants who could come from each country. The law was largely directed against eastern and southern Europeans. It also barred all Asians except Filipinos, who were American nationals as long as the Philippine Islands were an American possession. Here, for example, is how the law affected Polish immigration in the 1920s. Ninety-five thousand Poles immigrated to the United States in 1921. Between 1922 and 1924, the United States admitted about 28,000 Poles annually. From 1925 to 1930, the number was reduced to 8,000 a year. During the same period, the United States admitted about 45,000 Germans each year.

REMIGRATION AND THE DEPRESSION

The numbers of eastern Europeans who remigrated back to their homelands were always high. Perhaps as many as a third of the Hungarians and Poles who came to America before 1914 went back. However, only about 5 percent of the Jews from eastern Europe returned. Those who went back did so for several reasons. Some made enough money to buy land back home. Some found life in America too hard and lonely. Many had never intended to stay.

The Great Depression (1930–1941) was a period of severe hardship for many Americans. Millions were unemployed. Hundreds of thousands lost their homes and farms. The public's resentment of "foreigners" grew as the competition for jobs became stiffer. Many eastern European immigrants returned home so they could help or be helped by their families. For four years during the depths of the depression (1932 to 1935), more people left the United States than entered.

After World War I, many eastern Europeans joined the stream of immigrants returning home with earnings from America. These men are boarding a steamer leaving from New York.

THE RISE OF TYRANNY IN EUROPE

In 1933 Adolf Hitler officially assumed power in Germany. Hitler was the leader of the National Socialist German Workers (Nazi) Party. He took over a country that had been ravaged by debt, inflation, and economic depression. Hitler blamed German Jews for these economic conditions. His Nazi followers embarked on a campaign of persecution against the Jews. Jewish shops were wrecked, and many Jews lost their jobs. In 1935, the German government passed a series of laws called the Nuremberg Laws. These laws deprived Germany's 500,000 Jews of their citizenship and virtually all their rights. Hitler also persecuted other groups, such as labor and church leaders, Gypsies, and Communists. Thousands of people began to flee Germany during the 1930s to escape Nazi persecution.

During the same period, another ruthless tyrant, Joseph Stalin, was attempting to turn the Soviet Union into a major industrial power. His methods were brutal. Millions of peasants starved when he seized their land and forced them to work on state-owned farms. He murdered hundreds of thousands of Communist Party leaders, army officers, and cultural and academic leaders. These murders were called "purges." Stalin's purpose was to eliminate anyone who disagreed with him. With the help of his security police, Stalin terrorized the Soviet people into complete submission.

Stalin was particularly brutal to Soviet Jews. Many of those murdered in the purges were Jews who had risen to high levels of leadership in Soviet society. Stalin also terrorized people in countries occupied by the Soviet Union. For example, in 1940, Stalin's troops slaughtered more than 5,000 Lithuanians. Stalin shipped 32,000 Lithuanians to Siberia and deported 54,000 to Nazi Germany.

Adolf Hitler (1889–1945)

Joseph Stalin (1879–1953)

AMERICAN INDIFFERENCE

During the 1930s, the United States government continued to restrict immigration to the levels of the 1924 quotas. The country was still in the depths of the Great Depression. The government enacted many new programs to bring the depression to an end. However, it enacted no new laws to admit refugees from Nazi Germany. The nation was still in an anti-immigration mood. In addition, anti-Semitism was widespread in America in the 1930s. American Jews were commonly denied high-level jobs, and quotas limited their admission to the best colleges. Many of the early Communist leaders in Europe had been Jews. Some Americans believed that Jewish immigrants were Communist agents who wanted to destroy American democracy.

Since most refugees from Nazi Germany were Jews, many Americans felt little enthusiasm for letting them come to the United States. In 1939, some members of Congress introduced a bill to allow 20,000 children to be rescued from Nazi Germany. There was widespread support for the bill from government agencies and liberal organizations such as labor unions and Jewish organizations. Nevertheless, the bill was defeated after it was attacked by conservative groups. "The children are coming to be the shock troops of the revolution of tomorrow," said an opponent. "Every child is to be sent into a communist home and everyone who is supporting this measure is a communist."[1]

THE *ST. LOUIS*

The United States was not alone in refusing to admit Nazi refugees. Most other nations also refused to accept them. In May 1939, the Nazis allowed a German cruise liner, the *St.*

[1] *Source:* Barbara McDonald Stewart. *United States Government Policy on Refugees from NAZIism, 1933–1940* (New York: Garland), 1982, pp. 531–532.

The German liner *St. Louis* carrying German and Austrian Jewish refugees in 1939

Louis, to sail to Cuba carrying more than 900 German and Austrian Jewish refugees. When they arrived in Havana, the Cuban government refused to honor most of the refugees' visas. Turned away, the ship sailed up the coast of America. Off Miami Beach, Florida, the passengers could hear music from the big hotels. Both the United States and Canada turned the refugees away. The refugees had no choice but to return to Germany. Many of them were later killed by the Nazis. As Americans learned more about Nazi atrocities, public opinion and government policy did change a little. In 1944, near the end of the war, the government arranged for another ship, the *Henry Gibbins,* to bring about 1,000 Jewish and Christian refugees to America. Most of them later became American citizens.

SOME DID COME

In 1939, Great Britain and France declared war on Germany. America entered World War II in 1941. During the troubled times between 1933 and 1945, America admitted about 250,000 European refugees. They came not only from Germany but also from the countries Germany had conquered, such as Poland, Hungary, and Czechoslovakia.

Most of the adult refugees were middle class, well educated, and highly skilled. They were very useful to America during wartime. Some of these immigrants were scientists. The German physicist Albert Einstein was perhaps the most famous. Others included Lise Meitner (Austria), Leo Szilard and Edward Teller (Hungary), and Enrico Fermi (Italy). All these scientists helped America develop the atomic bomb.

The world-famous composer Béla Bartók came to the United States from Hungary in 1940. He barely subsisted on earnings from piano recitals and a few compositions and the assistance from a musicians' association. His health began to fail, and he died in poverty in New York City in 1945. Also from Hungary came the conductor George Szell and the playwright Ferenc Molnár.

Another famous refugee was Henry Kissinger, a German Jew who would become U.S. secretary of state.

Béla Bartók (1881–1945)

ETHNIC RELIEF ORGANIZATIONS

World War I had left much of Europe in ruins. In the United States, European immigrants formed hundreds of groups to help the people in their homelands recover after the war. Polish Americans formed several national federations or organizations to help their new country. One, the Alliance of Malopolski Clubs, founded in 1929, raised more than $500,000 in ten years. Lithuanian Americans, a small minority, raised $2 million after World War I by selling Lithuanian Freedom Loan bonds.

Some ethnic relief groups were also political. Hungarian American churches and social clubs sponsored rallies to protest the division of their homeland after World War I. The World Association of Estonians was founded in 1940 to oppose the Soviet occupation of Estonia.

American Jewish organizations performed spectacularly after World War I. During the 1930s, the American Jewish Congress organized a boycott of German goods and lobbied Congress on behalf of Jewish refugees. The Joint Distribution Committee raised nearly $80 million between 1939 and 1945. Most of the money was used to help people escape from Nazi Germany. The organizations offered much-needed sympathy and hope, as well as material aid.

Under the Immigration Act of 1924, immigrants to the United States had to prove that they could get by on their own. Usually this meant they had to have jobs or have relatives who would promise to support them. Many ethnic churches and relief groups helped new immigrants get jobs, find housing, and deal with the immigration authorities. After World War II, these groups played a major role in helping refugees come to America and start new lives. Many thousands of postwar immigrants would not have made it to America without their valuable help.

World War II

The United States entered World War II on December 7, 1941. By then, Europe had been ravaged by war for more than two years. Hitler's armies overran most of Europe. As the war progressed, Nazi persecution of the Jews turned into something much, much more horrifying—the Holocaust. Throughout Germany and in the German-occupied countries, Hitler constructed concentration camps, which were efficient killing factories where millions of men, women, and children could be starved, tortured, and murdered.

Historians estimate that Hitler killed 6 million Jews. He may have murdered as many as 5 million others—Communists; political, religious, and labor leaders; Gypsies; the mentally retarded; and homosexuals. In addition, he forced many thousands of people from occupied countries, such as Poland and Czechoslovakia, to work as slave laborers in Germany. The Soviet Union, although a major victim of Nazi barbarism, also displaced and enslaved thousands of people from occupied territories during World War II.

DISPLACED PERSONS

When World War II ended in 1945, millions of people were left stranded, homeless, and far from their countries and families. They were known as displaced persons (DPs). These people included survivors of the concentration camps and slave laborers from nearly every country in Europe. In addition, there were large numbers of Germans who had fled from the Soviet army. They had no money and no means of feeding or clothing themselves or returning home. Many were in very poor physical condition.

The Allies were faced with an enormous task: feeding, housing, and sorting out more than a million people. At first, they did it badly. Among 60,000 concentration camp survivors, several thousand died within a week after they were freed. The Allies housed DPs in barracks, airplane hangars, huts, stables—wherever there was room. Some DPs were even housed in the very concentration camps where they had been imprisoned. Worse, some former concentration camp guards were allowed to declare themselves DPs and were housed along with the survivors.

The Allies also adopted a policy of treating everyone alike, regardless of religion. This made conditions far worse for Jews. They had been treated more harshly than most others and needed more help. Volunteers who helped in the camps after the war were also ignorant of what the concentration camp survivors had endured. One volunteer, for example, complained that it was very difficult to get survivors to take showers. "Quite a few had to be forcefully pushed or carried in," he said.[1] He was apparently unaware that the Nazis had used showers to gas people.

Many of the DP camps were plagued by bad food, crime, and severe overcrowding. Gradually, conditions got better.

[1] *Source:* Leonard Dinnerstein. *America and the Survivors of the Holocaust* (New York: Columbia Univ. Press), 1982, p. 66.

A Polish family being interviewed in a DP camp after World War II

Jews were allowed to have their own camps. People set about learning new skills. Some even wrote books or learned a trade in the DP camps.

REDRAWING THE BOUNDARIES

Like World War I, World War II was a turning point in the history of eastern Europe. After the war, the four Allied powers—Great Britain, the United States, France, and the Soviet Union—established four zones in Germany. The three western zones became democratic West Germany. The Soviet zone became Communist East Germany.

In addition, the Soviet Union dominated most of eastern Europe. This included the Baltic republics of Lithuania, Latvia, and Estonia, which were annexed to the Soviet Union, Poland, Czechoslovakia, Romania, Hungary, Bulgaria, and, until 1961, Albania. Yugoslavia resisted total Soviet domination. All, however, soon became Communist nations. Many DPs did not want to return to countries that had fallen under Communist control.

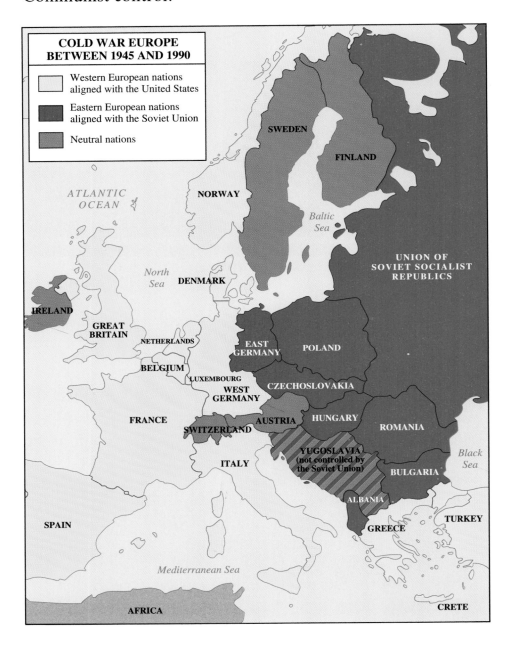

COLD WAR EUROPE
BETWEEN 1945 AND 1990

☐ Western European nations aligned with the United States

■ Eastern European nations aligned with the Soviet Union

▨ Neutral nations

ATLANTIC OCEAN

SWEDEN

FINLAND

NORWAY

Baltic Sea

North Sea

DENMARK

UNION OF SOVIET SOCIALIST REPUBLICS

IRELAND

GREAT BRITAIN

NETHERLANDS

BELGIUM

LUXEMBOURG

EAST GERMANY

POLAND

WEST GERMANY

CZECHOSLOVAKIA

FRANCE

SWITZERLAND

AUSTRIA

HUNGARY

ROMANIA

ITALY

YUGOSLAVIA (not controlled by the Soviet Union)

Black Sea

BULGARIA

ALBANIA

SPAIN

GREECE

TURKEY

Mediterranean Sea

AFRICA

CRETE

THE DISPLACED PERSONS ACT OF 1948

In 1945, as World War II ended, American immigration policy stayed the same. Many Americans remained anti-Semitic or anti-immigrant. Although there was sympathy for the victims of the war, many people believed that the victims should start new lives in their own countries, not in America. There was much debate in Congress about what to do about European refugees. In 1946, President Harry Truman issued a directive that allowed 40,000 refugees to immigrate to America. About 28,000 of them were Jews. Many more Jews went to Palestine, which, in early 1948, became the new Jewish state of Israel.

Three years after the war ended, the refugee policy of the United States changed drastically. The Soviet Union went from being an ally to being an enemy. The two countries entered a long period of "cold war." There was no actual fighting. Rather, it was a war of ideas, of democracy versus communism. American policymakers soon became more concerned with rescuing refugees from communism than with rescuing refugees from Nazism. They even recruited former Nazis to help them spy on the Soviet Union.

Partly as a result of the cold war, Congress passed the Displaced Persons Act of 1948, which allowed the United States to admit 400,000 DPs between 1948 and 1952. The act required all refugees to have jobs, housing, and sponsors waiting for them before they could immigrate. Some received help from family members or friends. Many more were sponsored by ethnic relief organizations and other voluntary agencies, such as churches and synagogues, the Red Cross, and the YMCA/YWCA. The law required that 30 percent of the refugees be farm workers and that 40 percent be from areas annexed by a foreign power. These requirements reduced the number of Nazi victims who could gain entry and favored refugees from communism.

THE DISPLACED PERSONS ACT OF 1950

In 1950, Congress revised the 1948 act, dropping the provisions involving farm workers and annexed areas. Altogether, 450,000 refugees came to America under these acts. One researcher calculated that about 140,000 of them were Jews. According to various estimates, 178,000 Poles, 45,000 Latvians, 30,000 Lithuanians, 16,000 Hungarians, and 12,000 Czechs immigrated to the United States between 1946 and 1954. Many of these people were Jewish but were counted by nationality rather than religion.

For the most part, the refugees were well-educated middle-class people who fit in well with American values and traditions. Some had serious problems adjusting at first. Their most difficult problem was learning English. Many refugees moved into ethnic communities established by earlier immigrants. These communities provided companionship and support to the new immigrants.

THE McCARRAN-WALTER ACT

By 1952, America was deeper in the grip of the cold war, and U.S. immigration policy continued to reflect an anti-Communist orientation. That year, Congress passed the McCarran-Walter Act. This immigration law seemed to keep the 1924 national quotas intact. It did, however, allow the government to get around the quotas in some cases. The new law allowed the government to continue using a provision of the Displaced Persons Act of 1948 called "quota mortgaging." This meant that refugees from communism could use up future years' quotas to immigrate to the United States. A small country such as Latvia soon used up centuries' worth of future quotas.

Another provision of the McCarran-Walter Act was "parole." This allowed the attorney general to admit an unlimited number of immigrants temporarily for emergencies or reasons "deemed strictly in the public interest." Between 1945 and

1980, more than 2 million people were admitted under various refugee acts and parole provisions. These immigrants included thousands of Hungarians, and later, hundreds of thousands of Cubans and Southeast Asians fleeing Communist regimes.

Another feature of the McCarran-Walter Act was family reunification. The law gave special preference to people wishing to immigrate to the United States who already had husbands, wives, parents, or other close relatives living in America. This provision enabled many immigrants who had come just before or right after World War II to bring their close relatives to the United States. Finally, the McCarran-Walter Act ended the bans that still existed against many immigrants from Asia.

IMMIGRATION IN THE 1950s AND 1960s

Beginning in the 1920s, the Soviet Union made it impossible for its citizens to emigrate legally. Soviet leaders reasoned that since the state had provided its citizens with education, homes, and jobs, the citizens owed it to the state to remain and work for their nation. To make sure they did, the USSR sent dissidents to camps that used barbed wire, dogs, watchtowers, and guards to keep them in. After World War II, the Communist governments of eastern Europe used the same means at their borders to keep people from leaving.

Barbed wire and guard towers appeared along the Czech-Austrian border after World War II.

By the 1950s, eastern Europe was a prison with 3,000 miles of bars. Its borders had become, in Winston Churchill's apt phrase, an "iron curtain." Still, every year a small trickle of people did manage to get out. Usually they escaped alone or in small groups. They walked across frozen wastelands or risked land mines and bullets in the back to escape. These escapees were called "defectors."

Many of these defectors settled in western European countries. By 1961, 3.5 million East Germans—20 percent of the population—had fled into West Germany. To keep more from leaving, the East German government erected a wall, called the Berlin Wall, to cut off the flow. The wall also cut off use of the subway as an escape route.

Some refugees found their way to America. Between 1951 and 1960, 918 Czechs, 9,985 Poles, 1,039 Romanians, 584 Russians, and, after the 1956 uprising, about 36,000 Hungarians immigrated to the United States. The numbers increased for some groups during the 1960s. About 53,000 Poles, 3,273 Czechs, and about 2,400 Russians came in the 1960s.

Sometimes a famous artist or athlete, allowed to perform in the West, simply refused to go back. Top Russian ballet stars Rudolf Nureyev and Mikhail Baryshnikov defected while on tour in the West—Nureyev in 1961 and Baryshnikov in 1974. Tennis superstar Martina Navratilova of Czechoslovakia also defected while on tour in 1975.

THE IMMIGRATION ACT OF 1965

In general, the U.S. government did more and more to help refugees during the 1950s. As the DP acts expired, Congress passed the Refugee Relief Act of 1953, which authorized 205,000 people to come to the United States over a two-and-a-half-year period. These refugees were not counted in the quotas for their homelands. However, the act helped only

European refugees and ignored Asians, chiefly Chinese, who were displaced by World War II and the cold war.

In 1965, Congress enacted a new immigration law. This law enabled people from all parts of the world to come to America. It finally eliminated the unfair quotas that dated from 1924. Instead, it imposed a ceiling of 20,000 persons per year for each country and limits for each hemisphere. The Western Hemisphere had an annual limit of 120,000, and the Eastern Hemisphere had an annual limit of 170,000. But since relatives of persons already in the United States could enter regardless of these numerical limitations, these numbers were largely meaningless. This new law opened the way for millions of refugees and immigrants to come to the United States from Asia and Latin America. Today most immigrants come from these areas instead of from Europe.

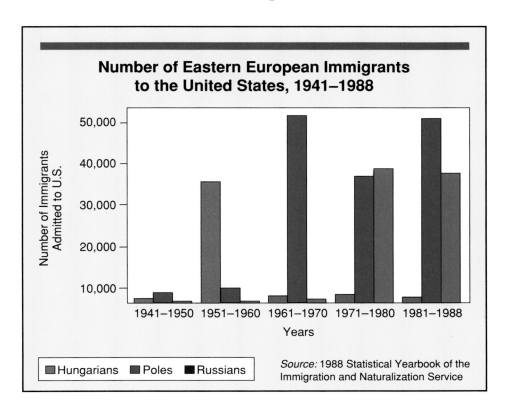

Number of Eastern European Immigrants to the United States, 1941–1988

Source: 1988 Statistical Yearbook of the Immigration and Naturalization Service

Poles, Hungarians, and Others

THE POLES

The first postwar Poles to come to America arrived in New York City in 1948 on an old troop carrier, the *General Black* (shown opposite). There were 831 men, women, and children who had spent years in concentration camps, slave labor camps, and displaced persons (DPs) camps. Some Poles dubbed the *General Black* the "Polish *Mayflower.*" Like the *Mayflower* Pilgrims, these Poles came to stay and make a new life in America. They were eager to adopt an American life-style. A great number of them had relatives and friends already living in the Polonias, or "Little Polands," of America's cities, such as Chicago, Buffalo, and Detroit. The new arrivals depended on these older hands to help them.

At the same time, many postwar immigrants were better educated than earlier immigrants had been. The older immigrants had been mainly peasant farmers. The postwar refugees were mainly city dwellers, managers, professionals, educators, and scientists. Many of the refugees were still moderately well off and brought some money with them. Others had been left penniless by the war.

Work Most postwar Polish immigrants were accustomed to working in white-collar jobs. They had not performed hard physical labor back home. Quite a few lied so they could qualify for immigration as farm laborers under the Displaced Persons Act of 1948. As a result, many Polish refugees found themselves working on ranches in Montana, farms in Kansas, and plantations in Louisiana. It was difficult for them to adapt to farm life. The southern planters in particular badly mistreated them. They were underpaid, underfed, and overworked. Within two or three years, nearly all left the farms to find better jobs in the cities.

The Polish DPs who settled in the cities also had a hard time. Many of them had to take menial jobs at first, such as working in factories, laundries, and restaurants. These were people

Polish DPs on their chicken farm in Connecticut, 1950

who had been teachers, writers, lawyers, and journalists in Poland. They felt humiliated and hurt. Nevertheless, within a few years, most had found better jobs working within their own professions again.

A New Kind of Immigrant The postwar refugees were very different from earlier Polish immigrants in many ways. The earlier immigrants had come for economic reasons, and many had intended to return to Poland. For that reason, they had resisted assimilation. They had tried to preserve their language and culture for when they went back home.

The new immigrants had gone through war, enslavement, and homelessness. Few had any desire to return to a war-torn and Communist Poland. Most knew that they were in America to stay, and they wanted to assimilate rapidly.

All these differences created conflicts between the new postwar refugees and the earlier immigrants. The refugees felt that the earlier immigrants were ignorant and uneducated. They thought these people spoke Polish badly. In addition, the newcomers felt the early immigrants knew little about Poland and Polish culture.

For their part, some of the earlier immigrants resented the newcomers. They saw the new refugees as members of the hated upper class of Polish society. It was this upper class, they felt, that had helped oppress the peasants for so long. The earlier immigrants felt the newcomers were trying to take over the leadership of the community they had built in America.

Both groups did have things in common, however. They both hated the Communists and desired a free and independent Poland once again. In addition, most Poles belonged to the Catholic church, and that provided a unifying bond for many, no matter what their class. Finally, Catholic welfare organizations, such as the Catholic Refugee Committee, played a large role in helping with the resettlement of refugees.

Bountiful America The Poles and other DPs were amazed by the wealth and bounty of America. After so many years of hunger and suffering, they had arrived in the richest country in the world. It was a land where stores were filled with food and clothing. Everyone seemed to have a car. Every home seemed to have a refrigerator and a washing machine. The cities throbbed with life. Thousands of people poured into the tall office buildings every day. Nightclubs and concert halls offered entertainment every night. Museums and libraries were open to the public for free or for only a small charge.

The newcomers were amazed by the freedom in America. There were no soldiers to terrify them or enslave them. In America, they soon realized, people in uniform were there to help them. They could say what they wanted. They could read their own newspapers in their own languages. They could attend their own churches and synagogues. Best of all, they could educate their children in America's public schools and choose the universities the children would attend.

Even Poles who have come in the 1980s are struck by the bounty of America. Jozef and Krystyna Patyna fled from Poland in 1983. Their first years in America were a great struggle. They both work in a factory and live very modestly. Here is what Krystyna says about how Poles view American life:

> *If we send a photo of our house back to Poland, people will think we are very rich. And to own a car is special. They see us dressed nice. They think we are in heaven and it is very easy to get rich in America. They don't understand how hard we work and how we sacrifice to save money.*
>
> Source: Al Santoli. *New Americans: Immigrants and Refugees in the U.S. Today—An Oral History* (New York: Viking Press, 1988), p. 81.

Members of the Polish Home Army Veterans Association of Chicago

Polish American Organizations   Like the earlier immigrants, the postwar Polish refugees were overwhelmingly Roman Catholic. They soon began attending services at established Polish Catholic churches. But many newcomers did not become involved in parish organizations and activities. The advent of a Polish Pope in 1978, however, brought a sense of kinship and pride to all Poles everywhere.

Many postwar refugees preferred to form their own organizations. Often these organizations reflected the immigrants' status as intellectuals and upper-class or middle-class Poles. The Polish Institute of Arts and Sciences was established in 1941 in New York City. This group sponsored many of the Polish writers and scientists who immigrated to the United States after the war. The Polish Nobility Association, founded in 1950, was open only to people who were once part of the Polish nobility. Poles also formed their own veterans groups and continued to be active in the Falcons, which were physical fitness and sports clubs. The Polish Home Army Veterans Association was made up of people who had fought in the Polish underground during the war.

Polish Americans on a visit to Warsaw in 1990

Ties to the Old Country   The Poles who came to America left behind a ravaged, war-torn country. As they prospered in America, the new immigrants began to send money and American goods to relatives and friends in Poland. This practice continues today. Poland never became a wealthy country under communism. People there have suffered repeatedly from shortages of food and consumer products.

Polish Americans have remained in close touch with Poland in other ways. They have remained staunchly anti-Communist and have followed recent events in Poland, which we mention later in the book. Many of them go back home for visits or to stay. Since the 1970s, Poland has encouraged tourism from the West. Travel agencies in the Polonias specialize in organizing vacation trips to Poland. In addition, more than 5,000 Polish Americans have retired to Poland since the 1970s.

THE HUNGARIANS

Hungarian immigrants came in two distinct groups immediately after World War II. About 16,000 Hungarian DPs entered the United States in 1945 and 1946. They were bureaucrats, army officers, lawyers, and managers. Many were nationalists, and almost all were anti-Communist.

The second group, consisting of about 10,000 Hungarians, came from 1947 to 1956. They were very different. Many of them had returned to Hungary after the war. A number were political leaders who had tried to work with the Communists who eventually took over the government. These refugees tended to be liberal or socialist. However, they were very unhappy with the harsh Communist rulers of their country.

The two groups were far apart politically. They agreed that they wanted an independent Hungarian homeland, but they disagreed on how to bring that about. Some members of the earlier group wanted to return to a lost world. They wanted to reestablish a monarchy in Hungary. The later group was more interested in establishing a democratic or republican form of government in which the people would have more of a say in running the government. Both groups had ties with earlier Hungarian immigrants in America. Many settled in established Hungarian communities in places such as Cleveland and New York City. But they did not mix much with one another.

The Hungarian Independence Movement The postwar Hungarian immigrants formed hundreds of organizations to promote Hungarian independence. Two of these groups were the Fraternal Association of Hungarian Veterans and the Hungarian Movement for Freedom. These were worldwide organizations that together recruited as many as 100,000 members during the 1950s.

After 1947, immigrants formed many anti-Communist organizations. One, the Hungarian National Committee (HNC),

In March 1848, Hungary revolted against its rulers.
On March 15, 1949, Hungarian Americans in New York
including film star Ilona Massey (left of wreath),
commemorate Hungarian Independence Day.

included a large number of former Hungarian political leaders. It was regarded by many as a sort of Hungarian government in exile.

Although these organizations started out as nationalist groups, most of them soon became cultural and social groups. They provided a place where postwar Hungarian Americans could meet to socialize and discuss common problems.

The Hungarian Revolution In October 1956, the Hungarian people revolted against their Soviet oppressors. They overthrew the Communist government and installed a new government that promised free elections and other democratic reforms. The new government lasted only a few days before Soviet tanks rolled into Budapest, the capital of Hungary, and crushed the uprising. As the world watched, thousands of brave Hungarian "freedom fighters" battled the tanks with guns and homemade bombs. In the end, 25,000 Hungarians were killed in the fighting.

During the turmoil, 200,000 Hungarians fled across a briefly opened border to freedom in Austria. Many walked across an icy swamp separating the two countries. Whole families hid from Soviet border patrols that were hunting them down with dogs and guns. Most of the 200,000 refugees settled in western European countries, but 36,000 came to the United States.

A Soviet army armored car destroyed by Hungarian "freedom fighters" using homemade bombs

Many of the escapes in 1956 were dramatic. Thomas Blatt was twenty-three years old and a college graduate when the revolution broke out. Years later he remembered what happened:

> *The whole thing started at our university. The uprising was a completely spontaneous matter. For a few days, after October 23rd, we thought the uprising might succeed. . . . On November 9th we realized it was all over, and on November 13th we left. . . .*

Thomas and his friends made their way to within a few miles of the Austrian border, near the railroad tracks.

> *I started toward them when suddenly there is this guy with a machine gun. I offered him all the money I had. So the guy said, "All right. It is five miles to the border and you have forty-five minutes because in about forty-five minutes the Orient Express will come. When it comes, you either climb up the railroad embankment, in which case you will be captured, or you let the train run over you."*
>
> *So we started to run along the tracks. We passed about one hundred and fifty people. Apparently he had let everybody through. We ran like crazy till we were totally dead and finally fell down onto the Austrian side of the border. Three more people came. Then came the train. Then nobody came. We barely made it. That's how I got out. . . .*
>
> Source: Adapted from June Namias, *First Generation: In the Words of Twentieth-Century American Immigrants* (Boston: Beacon Press, 1987), pp. 144–145.

The 56ers   Many Hungarians had expected the United States to step in and help them fight the Soviets. They were disappointed when America did nothing; such an action might have led to nuclear war. However, the courage of the freedom fighters aroused the sympathy of the American public. President Dwight Eisenhower used the parole provision of the McCarran-Walter Act to let Hungarians in. The 36,000 refugees who came to America received a warm welcome. An old army post in New Jersey, Camp Kilmer, was reopened and used to house the refugees. Volunteer groups and government agencies helped them find homes and jobs.

Most of the Hungarians who came in 1956 were young, single men and women. Two-thirds of them were male, and many were students. Very few of them were actual freedom fighters. They had left Hungary simply because they had an opportunity to escape.

They were different from the two groups of DPs who had come immediately after World War II. Many of them were well-trained technical workers. They had been educated by the Communist government.

The 56ers blended into American life almost immediately. The American economy was booming. The nation needed more skilled workers. The Hungarians' training and skills brought them good jobs. Many of them soon married Americans from other ethnic groups. Most of the 56ers were not especially political or nationalistic. They planned to stay and become Americans.

For several years, many of the 56ers had little to do with the established Hungarian American community. But in the 1970s and 1980s, they began to search out Hungarian American organizations. They had a new desire to share their native language and cultural heritage with their American-born children.

Hungarian American Culture   By the late 1940s, the sons and daughters of earlier Hungarian immigrants were already moving up into the middle class and out to the suburbs. As is true of virtually every immigrant group, second- and third-generation Hungarian Americans were far more American than Hungarian. Their primary language was English, and many had little interest in the culture and customs of their parents' native land.

Hungarian refugees of the 1956 revolution, like these folk dancers from Budapest, helped bring new life to the Hungarian American community.

The DPs and later the refugees of the 1956 revolution helped revitalize the Hungarian American community. Their new clubs and organizations, as well as the Hungarian American press, became centers for preserving Hungarian language and culture.

With the 1960s came a general revival of ethnic life, not only in the Hungarian American community but in others as well. People began once again to take an interest in their heritage and make efforts to understand and preserve it.

OTHER EASTERN EUROPEANS

Of course, Poles and Hungarians were not the only peoples who fled from the Nazis and Soviets after World War II. Many of the DPs who refused to go home were from the Baltic countries. These countries—Lithuania, Latvia, and Estonia— were annexed by the Soviet Union during the war. About 45,000 Latvians, 30,000 Lithuanians, and 10,000 Estonians immigrated to the United States under the displaced persons acts. When the Soviets took over Czechoslovakia in 1948, some 25,000 refugees came to America. Another 16,000 arrived after the "Prague spring," an unsuccessful uprising in 1968.

The experience of these immigrants was very similar to that of the Hungarians and Poles. Many settled in established ethnic communities and helped revitalize their communities. Most were well-educated, skilled workers who were able to find good jobs in America. Many of those counted as Poles, Hungarians, Czechs, and citizens of the Baltic states were Jews. These immigrants settled in Jewish communities rather than ethnic Christian communities.

From the Soviet Union

Since the cold war began in the late 1940s, thousands of people have immigrated to the United States from the Soviet Union, an ethnically diverse nation. This includes 85,000 Ukrainians and thousands of Belorussians (White Russians), Cossacks, and other Soviet citizens.

By far the largest ethnic group to come from the Soviet Union has been the Soviet Jews, who have been persecuted in eastern Europe by both church and state for centuries. Murderous mob attacks, called "pogroms," resulted in the deaths of thousands of Jews. The Communists, who opposed all religion, tried to force the Jews to give up their religion and ethnic identity. Jews were not allowed to speak Yiddish. Their synagogues were closed, and they were not allowed to practice their religion. As a result, many Soviet Jews today know little or nothing about their religion or heritage.

Soviet Jews are not allowed to practice Judaism, but they are not allowed to blend in with the rest of Soviet society either. Their identity papers identify them as Jews. They are barred from the best universities and high-level jobs. Only a few Soviet Jews are members of the Communist Party.

REFUSENIKS AND DISSIDENTS

In 1948, the nation of Israel was founded in the land of Palestine. For the first time in centuries, the Jews had a country to call their own. Many Holocaust survivors chose to go to Israel after the war. Soviet Jews also began to look to Israel as a place where they too could be free.

However, the Soviet government made it very difficult for Jews to leave the country. Typically, Jews or any other Soviet citizens who wished to leave had to fill out dozens of applications to do so. Usually, they were turned down and had to try again and again. These people were called "refuseniks." Just applying to leave often cost Soviet citizens their jobs, apartments, and friends. Some refuseniks were dissidents. These were Soviet citizens who were very outspoken against the Soviet government. Many dissidents were imprisoned, placed in mental institutions, or exiled to Siberia.

Natan Sharansky, prominent Soviet mathematician and refusenik, was finally able to leave the Soviet Union for Israel in 1987. His wife, Avital Sharansky, spent years lobbying around the world for his release.

U.S. POLICY AND DETENTE

Despite all the difficulties placed in their way, about 90,000 people, mostly Jews, were able to emigrate from the Soviet Union between 1966 and 1982. One of the major reasons they were allowed to leave was that they were supported by the U.S. government.

From 1972 to 1980, the United States and the USSR were said to be in a period of "détente." This was a partial thawing or relaxation of the cold war. The Soviet Union wanted to increase its trade with the United States. The United States, in turn, wanted the government of the Soviet Union to treat its citizens more humanely. Under pressure from the United States, the Soviet Union allowed thousands of refuseniks to emigrate.

At first, the Soviet government continued to make things difficult for the refuseniks. In 1972, for example, it tried to impose a hefty "education tax" on those wishing to leave the country. The tax was supposed to repay the government for the education the refuseniks had received. This tax met with such an outcry from American leaders that the Soviet Union soon dropped it.

In 1975, the Soviet Union signed the Helsinki Accords, a European military security pact. One of the provisions of the pact required the Soviet Union to recognize that its citizens were entitled to basic human rights, such as freedom of speech, freedom of religion, and the right to emigrate. The Soviet Union never complied fully with that provision. However, the following year, Congress approved the Jackson-Vanik Amendment. This was a law requiring the Soviet Union to relax its emigration restrictions in order to get several favorable trade concessions from the United States. The amendment kept the pressure on the Soviet Union to allow Soviet Jews to emigrate.

"THE EVIL EMPIRE"

During President Jimmy Carter's administration (1976–1980), Carter stressed human rights in his foreign policy. He continued to pressure the Soviet Union to allow Soviet Jews and other Soviet dissidents to emigrate. In 1977, the Soviet Union allowed 16,000 Jews to leave. In 1978, the number reached 29,000.

Then, in 1979, the Soviet Union invaded Afghanistan. Its purpose was to reimpose a Communist government on the people of Afghanistan. Détente came to an end, and relations with the United States turned sour. President Carter ordered the United States to boycott the 1980 Olympics, which were held in Moscow. When President Ronald Reagan took office in 1981, he called the Soviet Union "the Evil Empire." During this period, the Soviet Union greatly reduced the number of people it allowed to leave the country. By 1983, the number had fallen to 1,314. The following year, only 894 were allowed to emigrate.

A Soviet helicopter on surveillance in Afghanistan following the invasion

Russian Jews arriving in Israel

THE UNITED STATES AND ISRAEL

When Israel became a Jewish nation in 1948, it adopted the "law of return." This law provided that any Jew, anywhere in the world, was welcome to immigrate to Israel. In the 1960s and early 1970s, nearly all the Jews who were allowed to leave the Soviet Union went to Israel. Then, starting in the late 1970s, the tide changed, and most of them started to come to the United States.

The Soviet Union requires all Soviet Jewish emigrants to apply for visas to Israel. They are flown to Vienna, Austria, where they are processed by Jewish agencies. Those who choose the United States say it is a bigger country with greater opportunities. They say there is less bureaucracy, religious extremism, and threat of war in the United States than there is in Israel.

RESETTLEMENT IN THE UNITED STATES

About 430,000 Jews left the Soviet Union from the mid-1960s to 1990, according to the Hebrew Immigrant Aid Society. An estimated 180,000 have immigrated to America. Nearly 50,000 of them have settled in New York City. Soviet Jews have also settled in many other cities.

At first, the immigrants receive a great deal of help and support from various Jewish synagogues and agencies, such as the Joint Distribution Committee and other national Jewish groups. They also receive help from family members and friends who immigrated earlier.

Nevertheless, Soviet immigrants face a lot of problems. They come from a society that has given them everything: education, jobs, housing, medical care. In America, they are expected to make it largely on their own. It is difficult for them to learn to become self-reliant. They must also learn a new language and adapt to a new culture. Many expected America to be an earthly paradise. They are appalled by the crime, poverty, and homelessness that exist here. Most do manage to adjust to life in America.

A recent Soviet immigrant, Alex Bushinsky, talks about his first few days in New York City:

> *In the first two days I hated the city. I lost job. I had no money. Definitely I hated it. I felt insecure, terrible. But in five days when I saw I could get a job just like that, I started to work and half a month later I realized my prospects were much better here. . . . This was a new world for me. There were so many things I did not have: language, American education; I was an American immigrant, a Russian, and still I got job.*
>
> Source: Thomas Kessner and Betty Boyd Caroli, *Today's Immigrants, Their Stories* (New York: Oxford Univ. Press, 1981), p. 181.

Brighton Beach   Many Soviet Jews and other Russian immigrants have settled in the Brighton Beach section of New York City. Brighton Beach was a run-down neighborhood along the Brooklyn seashore. The first Soviet immigrants settled there because it offered cheap housing. But the area also reminded many of the Soviets of the Russian city of Odessa, a seaport on the Black Sea.

Soon as many as 20,000 Russians, Jews and non-Jews alike, settled in Brighton Beach. They began to buy little shops and turned the area into a "Little Odessa." Most of the shop signs are in the Russian, or Cyrillic, alphabet, and spoken Russian fills the air. Many Russians have also settled in the Forest Hills, Washington Heights, and Riverdale sections of New York City. Some Soviet Jews live in religious communities in Brooklyn.

Russian Americans out for a stroll in Brighton Beach, New York

Jobs One of the changes that Soviet immigrants find difficult to accept is the idea that they must start at the bottom and work their way up in a job or career. In the Soviet Union, for many people their first job is the job they keep all their working lives. Many immigrants are well educated. They worked as doctors, engineers, and scientists in the Soviet Union. Within two or three years, most immigrants are able to find better jobs.

Businesses Many Soviet immigrants want to own their own businesses when they come to the United States. However, they usually know little or nothing about how to run an American business. They do not know how to borrow money, do their taxes, keep books, or order and market goods. Some

An enterprising Russian American has opened a new business in Brighton Beach.

government and social service agencies offer lectures and seminars to teach new business owners these skills.

Adjustment to American Life   In 1981, the Council of Jewish Federations conducted a study of 900 Soviet Jews who had immigrated to the United States. Three-fourths of those studied had arrived less than two years earlier. Most of them had come in families. Eighty percent of the men and 57 percent of the women were working full-time. The vast majority were working in white-collar or skilled jobs.

When they were asked why they had left the Soviet Union, nearly half cited anti-Semitism in the USSR. The biggest problems they mentioned were learning English, finding a good job, being separated from family members, and making enough money.

Overall, most of those surveyed were fairly happy and satisfied in their jobs. They felt that their housing, standard of living, and lives as Jews were better in America. The study also found that over time, the immigrants' incomes rose and their dependence on welfare and social services declined steadily.

According to the study, many immigrants rated cultural activities as being worse in the United States. They complained that the music, ballet, and opera available to them in America were inferior to what they had enjoyed in the Soviet Union and cost much more.

The study found that older immigrants more closely identified themselves as Jews than did younger ones. Three-quarters of them, however, said they wanted their children to have good Jewish educations. Just the act of immigrating has caused an identity crisis for some Soviet Jews. One said, "The paradox is that in Russia I was a Jew and now I am a Russian." In fact, many of those surveyed said they preferred to be called "Russian Americans" or "American Jews" rather than "Soviet Jews."

RECENT EVENTS AND LIFE TODAY

Gorbachev—Perestroika and Glasnost In 1985, Mikhail Gorbachev became the leader of the Soviet Union. He soon set about reforming the nation's economy and government. His economic reforms were referred to as *perestroika,* or "restructuring." His political reforms were called *glasnost,* or "openness." Gorbachev's reforms set the stage for dismantling the Communist system not only in the Soviet Union but throughout eastern Europe.

In 1989, the Soviet government conducted the first free elections ever held in the Soviet Union. The Soviet people now have much more freedom of speech, religion, and the press than they have ever had. Gorbachev brought the war in Afghanistan to an end. He released many imprisoned dissidents and refuseniks. Since 1987, the number of people who have been allowed to emigrate to other countries has increased significantly. Eleven thousand were allowed to leave in 1987, and 19,000 in 1988. Gorbachev's reforms have been so sweeping that many in America and the Soviet Union now say the cold war is over.

Events of 1989 Gorbachev's reforms opened the door for revolutionaries to overthrow their governments. During 1989, reform or non-Communist governments took over in Hungary, Romania, Bulgaria, and Czechoslovakia.

In Poland, the once banned labor union Solidarity now runs the country. Only a few years ago, it was banned by the Polish government and its leaders were imprisoned. The American people greatly supported Solidarity and its leader, Lech Walesa, winner of the 1983 Nobel Prize for Peace. He and new Czech president Vaclav Havel have addressed the U.S. Congress. In late 1990 Walesa became president of Poland.

Perhaps most startling of all has been the reunification of East and West Germany. When hundreds of thousands of East Germans fled west through Hungary in 1989, the East German

Mikhail Gorbachev

government tore down the hated Berlin Wall and allowed people to emigrate freely. On October 3, 1990, the two countries reunited as a new democratic Germany.

Changes in U.S. Policy   The reforms taking place in eastern Europe have caused the United States to change its policy toward Soviet refugees. Earlier, in the Refugee Act of 1980, Congress had defined a refugee as someone who has "a well-founded fear of being persecuted." However, since so many democratic reforms have occurred in the Soviet Union, the United States now feels that Soviet Jews need no longer fear persecution. Many Soviet Jews are afraid, however, that the Soviet reforms, which have led to demands for independence in Lithuania, Latvia, Estonia, the Ukraine, and other Soviet republics, will also result in increased anti-Semitism.

In 1989, the United States began to tighten the restrictions on the number of Soviet Jews who could immigrate to America. That year the government issued about 43,000 visas to Soviet emigrants, although many thousands more had applied. The United States argued that it could take only a

Germans in Berlin celebrate the destruction of the Berlin Wall.

limited number of Soviet refugees and that the rest should go to other countries, such as Canada, Australia, and Israel. At the same time, Israel pressured the United States to stop accepting Soviet Jews so they would be forced to go to Israel instead.

CONTRIBUTIONS TO AMERICAN LIFE

When eastern European refugees first started coming to America after World War II, many Americans feared they would become public burdens. As it turned out, far from being a burden, most immigrants have contributed enormously to American life. The war brought thousands of scientists, intellectuals, writers, musicians, and teachers. It also brought countless skilled workers and professionals whose work has enriched the lives of millions of Americans.

From Poland came Dr. Ludwik Gross, whose cancer research has led to more effective ways to treat leukemia and malignant tumors. Mieczyslaw Bekker also came from Poland during World War II. He created the rover vehicle used by American astronauts to explore the moon.

In the last twenty years, thousands of actors, dancers, painters, sculptors, film directors, and musicians have come from the Soviet Union and other eastern European countries. They wanted to find the artistic freedom they were denied under communism. Their talents have greatly enriched American theater, music, and film.

The new immigrants from eastern Europe have revitalized their ethnic communities in the United States. They have kept alive their languages, customs, foods, holidays, and music. Today, Americans enjoy polkas, Pulaski Day parades, borscht, ballets and operas, pierogi, folk and classical music, art, goulash, and many other things that were brought here by eastern Europeans.

Mikhail Baryshnikov

At the age of twenty-six, Mikhail Baryshnikov was the star of the Soviet Union's Kirov Ballet. He was upset, however, because the Soviet government told him when, where, and how to dance. He had to decide between love for his homeland and artistic freedom. On June 24, 1974, he defected while he was in Canada performing with the Bolshoi Ballet.

Baryshnikov was born in Riga, Latvia, in 1948. He began to study dance at age twelve and moved to Leningrad three years later to study with the Kirov Ballet. At the age of eighteen he became a soloist, and soon was a star in the Soviet Union.

After he defected, Baryshnikov came to the United States and joined the American Ballet Theatre. He later danced with the New York City Ballet and his own Baryshnikov & Co. From 1980 to 1989, he was the director of the American Ballet Theatre.

Baryshnikov has appeared in two films, *The Turning Point* and *White Nights*, as well as in several television programs. His dancing and worldwide fame have made the ballet more popular with the American public.

Zbigniew Brzezinski

Zbigniew Brzezinski was born in Warsaw in 1928. He came to the United States in the early 1950s. His father was a Polish diplomat stationed in Canada when World War II started. The Brzezinski family settled permanently in Canada after the war rather than return to Communist Poland.

Brzezinski earned a Ph.D. from Harvard University in 1953. He became a member of the Harvard faculty and then the faculty of Columbia University, where he pursued his lifelong interest, the study of communism. In 1961, Brzezinski became an adviser to President-elect John F. Kennedy. Throughout the 1960s and 1970s, he continued to teach and write scholarly books on communism. From time to time, he also acted as a presidential adviser. When Jimmy Carter was elected President in 1976, he appointed Brzezinski to head the National Security Council, a cabinet-level position. Brzezinski was only the second Polish American to hold such a high-ranking position in the U.S. government.

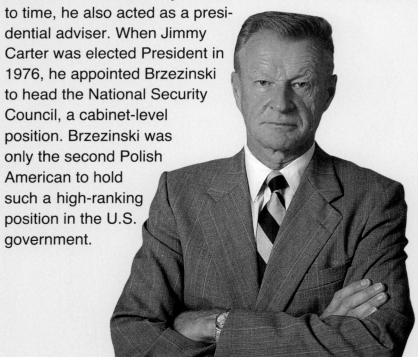

Galina Vishnevskaya

Galina Vishnevskaya is an opera singer who became a star in her native Russia before defecting to the United States in 1975. She was born in Leningrad in 1926. She won a contest to become a trainee with the Bolshoi Opera Company in Moscow in 1952. Three years later, she married Mstislav Rostropovich, one of the world's best-known cellists.

During the 1950s and 1960s, Vishnevskaya toured throughout the Soviet Union and Europe. In 1961, at the height of the cold war, she was invited to sing at the Metropolitan Opera House in New York City. Vishnevskaya toured the United States three times in the 1960s.

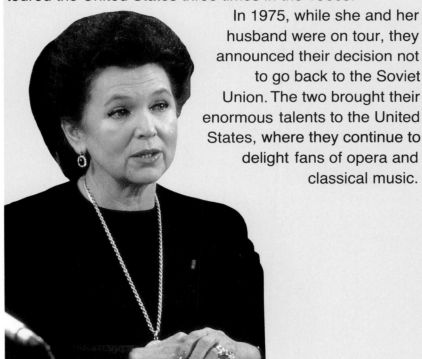

In 1975, while she and her husband were on tour, they announced their decision not to go back to the Soviet Union. The two brought their enormous talents to the United States, where they continue to delight fans of opera and classical music.

Martina Navratilova

World-famous tennis star Martina Navratilova was born in Prague, Czechoslovakia, in 1956. At the age of sixteen, she was ranked the number one women's tennis player in Czechoslovakia. Navratilova began to play on the international tennis circuit. She visited the United States and loved it. She also wanted to play tennis without being under the restrictive eye of Czech officials. At the age of eighteen, she defected to the United States.

I could look around and see that the Czech people weren't happy. There was a growing sadness, a melancholia. . . . I began to realize there was no room in that system to make decisions about my life. If I stayed, I belonged to them. My life would never be my own.

Navratilova became a U.S. citizen in 1981. She has won the Wimbledon singles title nine times since 1978—the only person ever to do so. She has also won the U.S. Open four times and the French Open twice.

Source: Martina Navratilova, with George Vecsey. Martina (New York: Knopf, 1985), p. 126.

THE FUTURE

America's eastern European immigrants have made good lives for themselves in their new land. Most have become citizens. They share the democratic values of America and contribute much to its spiritual and cultural life. As with other immigrant groups, their children and grandchildren are likely to become more and more Americanized.

As democratic changes continue in eastern Europe, many immigrants will be able to end their exile from their homelands. The eastern European nations will allow much more trade, tourism, and contact with western Europe and America. They may even become partners with western Europe in the European Economic Community (EEC).

Eastern European immigrants will be able to renew old ties with relatives and friends back home. They will be able to travel to their homelands, and people from eastern Europe will be able to travel to America. More eastern European students will be able to attend American universities. Gorbachev has already allowed a few Soviet students to study in the United States. More American students may be able to go to eastern European universities as well.

As change comes to eastern Europe, it is hard for some people to let go of the past as they experience feelings of uncertainty about the future. Andrzej Drawicz, a fifty-seven-year-old Polish professor of Russian literature and a onetime political prisoner, put it this way:

Sometimes I feel a bit nostalgic for the old times, but this is balanced by the fact that things are working out for the better. We wanted to be responsible for our fate, and now we are.

Source: U.S. News and World Report, July 31, 1989, pp. 30–32.

A Polish American dance troupe

Sources

Bradbury, John. *Eastern Europe: The Road to Democracy*. New York: Franklin Watts, 1990.

Bradbury, John. *Soviet Union: Will Perestroika Work?* New York: Franklin Watts, 1989.

Daniels, Roger. *Coming to America: A History of Immigration and Ethnicity in American Life*. New York: Harper Collins, 1990.

Dinnerstein, Leonard. *America and the Survivors of the Holocaust*. New York: Columbia Univ. Press, 1982.

Himmelfarb, Milton, ed. *American Jewish Yearbook, 1980 and 1986*. Philadelphia: The Jewish Publication Society of America.

Kessner, Thomas, and Betty Boyd Caroli. *Today's Immigrants, Their Stories: A New Look at the Newest Americans*. New York: Oxford Univ. Press, 1981.

Kuniczak, W. S. *My Name Is Million: An Illustrated History of Poles in America*. Garden City, N.Y.: Doubleday & Company, Inc., 1978.

Namias, June. *First Generation: In the Words of Twentieth-Century American Immigrants*. Boston: Beacon Press, 1987.

Navratilova, Martina, with George Vecsey. *Martina*. New York: Alfred A. Knopf, 1985.

Roberts, Elizabeth. *Europe 1992: The United States of Europe?* New York: Gloucester Press, 1990.

Rossel, Seymour. *The Holocaust: The Fire That Raged*. New York: Franklin Watts, 1989.

Santoli, Al. *New Americans: Immigrants and Refugees in the U.S. Today—An Oral History*. New York: Viking Press, 1988.

Simon, Rita J. *New Lives: The Adjustment of Soviet Jewish Immigrants in the United States and Israel*. Lexington, Mass.: Lexington Books, 1985.

Stewart, Barbara McDonald. *United States Government Policy on Refugees from NAZIism, 1933–1940*. New York: Garland Publishing, Inc., 1982.

Thernstrom, Stephan, ed. *Harvard Encyclopedia of American Ethnic Groups*. Cambridge, Mass.: Harvard Univ. Press, 1980.

Vardy, Steven B. *The Hungarian-Americans*. Boston: Twayne Publishers, 1985.

Index